You are Stardust:

Little Adventures in Perspective

Thanks to Ellie Underdown and Emma Boardman
for your encouragement :)

Copyright © 2020 Lisa Murray

Illustrations by Iryna Smirnova

ISBN: 9798566565576

www.helloworldpress.co.uk

Dedicated to Mum and Dad

~

'93 percent stardust,
with souls made of flames,
we are all just stars that have people names.'

(Nikita Gill)

~

You are a cosmic work of art.

'Everything we see is a perspective, not the truth.'

(Marcus Aurelius)

Life is how we decide to look at it.

And we always have the freedom to choose.

Underneath whatever may be happening, lies a stillness, a space, a moment.

A moment which contains within it a whole world of possibility.

An opportunity to shift, change, release, expand, to see things anew.

Sometimes we just need a little help to see things differently. To step back and see the bigger picture.

This book is a collection of moments.

Moments to shift perspective; from our inner selves to outer space; from fear to love; from less than to more than enough.

Each of these quotes and realisations came to me when I needed them – when I was looking for a spark of inspiration, a hug of reassurance, a sign that everything was OK. They filled me with appreciation and helped me realise I wasn't alone.

We're all in it together :)

Courage

The word 'courage' comes from the Latin root 'cor' which means 'heart'.

Courage is simply living from your heart.

'When we look out into space, we are looking out into our own origins, because we are truly children of the stars. And written into every atom and every molecule of our bodies is the entire history of our universe, from the big bang to the present day.

Our story is the story of the universe. Every piece of everyone, everything you love, everything you hate, and the thing you hold most precious, was assembled by the forces of nature in the first few minutes of the life of the Universe. Transformed in the hearts of stars, or created in their fiery deaths.'

(Brian Cox, Wonders of the Universe)

Keep it unreal.

It's so easy for another day to pass with the same thoughts, actions, expectations, attachments ... what if today instead of keeping it real, you keep it unreal?

What if you go outside the edges. Feel the surreal. Marvel a moment at the sheer bizarreness of the world, and the fact you're alive.

If you let go of the things you 'expect' to see or happen today, new moments or realities can crystallize.

Embrace the bizarre, keep it unreal :)

'If you want to build a ship, don't drum up people to collect wood and don't assign them tasks and work, but rather teach them to long for the endless immensity of the sea.'

(Antoine de Saint-Exupéry)

Behind everything is a deeper yearning, a swell of the heart; a call which when answered will show you how appreciated and needed you are.

Ever tried having a conversation with the universe? If you have a question you want answered, why not try a little cosmic chat?

Find a quiet space, take a deep breath and feel your feet grounded on the earth. Let your awareness soften. Gently bring your awareness to your heart and become aware of any energy there. Imagine it radiating out. Radiating out to connect with the universe – expanding further to the stars, to the perfect stillness of the infinite.

Then allow a question to come to your mind. Silently, offer that question to the universe. Surrender. Let it go. Then become aware of any words, images or sensations which may appear. There are no wrongs or rights, just trust whatever comes up for you.

Et voilà, I hope you enjoyed this little cosmic experiment!

There is no body in the world that is more than 7 years old.

98% of the atoms in your body were not there a year ago. Your skin is new every month. You make a new skeleton every 3 months. You have a new stomach lining every 4 days, new liver every 6 weeks, and new lungs every 3 weeks.

Every 7 years you are essentially a new person.

'Tears are words which need to be written.'

(Paulo Coelho)

Feeling upset or crying doesn't mean you have gone 'backwards'. Or 'failed' to be positive.

Crying can free you.

When the force of the sadness, hurt or frustration has passed, you are left with a new truth.

And this is what inspires change, growth, empathy. This is what creates the greatest works of art and reminds us that we are never alone in feeling this way.

The incredible emptiness of an atom.

99.99999999999% of an atom is nothingness. If you could squeeze all the empty space out of all the atoms in all the people in the world, you could fit the human race in the volume of a sugar cube.

Suddenly it seems hard to take things too seriously :)

One small step for man, one giant leap for mankind.

Every little step you take towards something you love, something which excites you, inspires you, which makes you feel alive, however small – that little step can also be felt by the people around you, the people you meet, radiating out to touch the whole world.

Making yourself happy is the opposite of selfish.

Everyone knows that curiosity killed the cat. Except …

The original proverb was actually 'care killed the cat'. 'Care' meaning 'worry'– so the proverb was actually 'worry killed the cat'!

For all this time we've been hearing this little warning against curiosity when curiosity is what can make us feel most alive.

When we're curious we give ourselves permission to go off the beaten path; to explore, see things anew and open up to new possibilities.

'Satisfaction of one's curiosity is one of the greatest sources of happiness in life.'

(Linus Pauling)

We are only ever one thought away from a new experience of being alive.

If people on a planet 65 million light years away looked at Earth with a powerful enough telescope, they would see dinosaurs.

Light takes time to travel. Looking at anything is tantamount to looking back in time. And the further away it is, the further back in time you see.

Assuming you are about 2 feet or so from this page, then you are reading this sentence as it was about 2 nanoseconds earlier. If you look at the moon, the light left it about a second ago. For the sun, it is closer to 8 minutes.

We are watching imprints of the past.

I choose.

Two of the most powerful words that can be spoken.

Every moment, every day you can choose how you want to feel.

Think it to yourself, say it out loud…'I choose ...'

Whatever you want! I choose to have fun today, I choose to be kind to myself, I choose to be free, I choose to do things which make me smile, I choose to love deeply …

Whatever will make you feel good.

'I choose' opens the door to a little shift – a shift towards empowerment and possibilities.

'You are never alone or helpless. The force that guides the stars guides you too.'

(Shrii Shrii Anandamurti)

'Anxiety is the dizziness of freedom.'

(Søren Kierkegaard)

The world is wide open to us, full of possibilities and opportunities.

Sometimes it's just the thought of making a choice that is overwhelming.

Even if we consider all the possible outcomes, weigh up the 'best' choice, think of all the infinite possibilities … we really don't know until we just make the decision.

Then we're free in that moment. Then there is just living that decision; no rights or wrongs, just experiences, and moving forward to the next liberating moment.

You can shape the world without anyone knowing your name.

There are a cast of people you are unlikely to have heard of – those behind the scenes who supported, loved, and inspired some of the greatest artists and minds in history.

Behind every great person is someone who helped them believe they could do it.

Don't underestimate what a difference you can, and have made, with a word of encouragement.

10 billion miles (and counting).

Voyager 1. The first man-made object to journey into the uncharted void of interstellar space.

Made of silicon and aluminium and with less processing power than an electronic key fob.

The pluckiest underdog of all time (and space).

'Our fears are like dragons guarding our deepest treasures.'

(Rainer Maria Rilke)

'If you want to find the secrets of the universe, think in terms of energy, frequency and vibration.'

(Nikola Tesla)

We are energy. Although our body, and everything in the world appears to be material, it's an illusion.

We think everything we touch is solid, but it's mostly empty space.

However this emptiness, this 'nothing' – is every-thing.

It's what underlies the universe, it's the essence of every life form, this untouchable but knowable life force.

You can feel it flowing through you now, beating your heart, circulating through you and throughout the universe.

We are never fixed or stuck, we are dynamic.

Energy never dies, only transforms, and we are vibrational beings full of infinite potential.

In order to be who you were born to become, life couldn't have happened any other way.

'Our contemplations of the cosmos stir us. There is a tingling in the spine, a catch in the voice, a faint sensation, as if a distant memory of falling from a great height. We know we are approaching the grandest of mysteries.'

(Carl Sagan)

It's not you, it's us :)

Most of what we think is wrong with ourselves is simply the human condition.

Whatever you feel, step back from thinking 'I' and instead try 'we.'

All these emotions are simply part of a shared human experience. An experience which is meant to be rich, colourful and full of contrasts. We are meant to feel it all. Each emotion arises to help us, to show us something, to help us work out what we do want and what we don't want.

We're all in it together.

Enjoy your humanity.

There have been over a 100 billion people to have lived and died on planet Earth but there has never been, and will never be, another you.

In the Amazon, the Pirahã people have no history or descriptive words. They live without time or numbers, without colours or a shared past.

They don't speak of the past or the future – instead, they have a concept and expression – Xibipíío – current experience. Only now exists or is of interest to them.

In the present moment, all we have is freedom.

And all we have is the present moment.

The past is memory, the future is imagination.

There is only now.

Now is where we have the freedom to create anything and feel everything – to begin again.

Everything we do comes from a place of either love, or fear.

It's more effective when you don't try as much.

We're conditioned to believe we need to struggle, push, grasp for everything we want.

But next time, instead of holding on so tight, try loosening your grip.

Instead of searching out there, try turning gently inward.

Instead of doing something, *anything,* because it feels more proactive, try remaining still until an action or inclination draws you to move forward.

In Taoism, there is a concept 'Wu Wei' – the principle of not forcing in anything that you do.

Not swimming against the waves but allowing the sea to still. Then surrendering, being carried along with the flow which feels right in that moment.

There are more cells in our body than there are stars in a thousand Milky Ways.

'It began as a mistake.'

(Charles Bukowski)

This could be the first line in a new adventure in your life.

If we don't 'fail' or experiment, we will never know what we're capable of.

Universe.

Uni = one, verse = song.

We all play a part in the grandest symphony.

Ichi-go Ichi-e (*Japanese*):

an encounter which happens only once in a lifetime, reminding us to treasure every moment.

'It has been said that if a man raises a finger, he creates a corresponding albeit infinitesimal displacement in the stars, such is the absolute and all extending link between everything that is.'

(source unknown)

There is no separation.

Anytime we feel lost, small, or alone, it is because we have forgotten we belong to each other.

'I've lived through some terrible things in my life, some of which actually happened.'

(Mark Twain)

'No experience has been too unimportant, and the smallest event unfolds like a fate, and fate itself is like a wonderful, wide fabric in which every thread is guided by an infinitely tender hand and laid alongside another thread and is held and supported by a hundred others.'

(Rainer Maria Rilke)

The afterglow of awe.

When we experience that moment of wonder, of clarity, as it all comes into sharp focus. Everything expands; as if we have discovered a secret, that we *know*, that another piece of the puzzle has fallen into place.

Then, it passes.

Softens.

Becoming more like a warm comforting hug, an afterglow.

And the beauty is we are free to begin the search again.

PERSPECTIVE
SHIFTS & TIPS

~

ONE-LINERS

For an instant perspective shift!

- ✧ The atoms in your right hand might have come from a different star than those in your left hand
- ✧ You will be someone's best thing
- ✧ There is no such thing as a mistake
- ✧ Everything is temporary
- ✧ You are a story you tell yourself
- ✧ This isn't happening to me, it is happening for me
- ✧ What a nice thought that some of the best days of our lives haven't happened yet
- ✧ Don't take your thoughts so personally
- ✧ No one knows enough to be a pessimist
- ✧ What other people think of you is none of your business

QUICK QUESTIONS

Lost perspective? Ask yourself …

- ✧ How do I really feel just now?
- ✧ Will this matter in 5 years' time?
- ✧ Do I really need to think about this just now?
- ✧ Is this thought …
  - true?
  - helpful?
  - enjoyable?
- ✧ Where do I want to focus my energy and attention?
- ✧ How much time each day do I leave for the unknown? E.g. in amongst the same routine, tasks, repeated actions & tasks … How much space do I leave for new opportunities and experiences?
- ✧ What if there's not a 'wrong' path?

MOVE INTO A BETTER MOOD

Try taking a different stance!

Shake it off

As simple as it sounds. Shake any part of your body in any way you want (but ideally keep your feet on the floor so you're grounded). Imagine shaking off any frustrations, feelings, annoyances; shake off stress from your fingertips, shake off busy thoughts from your head … shake free any negative energy you don't want – shake it all off whilst enjoying the frenetic fun 'dog after a bath with no towel and no regrets' freedom of it all :)

Shift your state

Stand up. Stretch. Put your hands above your head in a celebratory fashion! Roll your shoulders back and down, chest out, boom taking care of business stance. Open your arms and hands as if you are excitedly receiving lots of amazing things you want.

Whatever you fancy doing! Just change things up for a few seconds. As well as the fact we tend to spend a large part of the day sitting, we also tend to repeat the same range of motions with our body. By moving in a slightly different way and playing around with embodying how we'd like to feel (e.g. a happy pose, a confident pose) we can release stuck energy (and thoughts) and shift to a healthier perspective.

Hand on heart

If you're feeling low, or lost, pause for a moment, and simply place your hand on your heart. Breathe gently, softly, deeply into your heart centre. Then say to yourself (in your mind or out loud) 'I choose love.' Repeat this to yourself until you feel it in your heart, and begin to feel yourself shift from fear, to your natural state of love.

Breathe it out

Breathe in for 4 seconds, hold for 2 seconds, then breathe out for 6 seconds.

If you find 6 seconds a long time, so long as you breathe out for longer than you breathe in, it's all good. When you exhale for even a few counts longer than you inhale, the vagus nerve (running from your neck down through your diaphragm to your abdomen) sends a signal to your brain to turn up your parasympathetic nervous system and turn down your sympathetic nervous system. Turning up relaxation and rest, turning down fight or flight.

DAILY DOSES OF PERSPECTIVE

Take whenever required!

- Theme tune

  Think of a song which makes you feel like a motherflipping baddass. The song you'd enter a boxing ring to. The song which instantly fills you with attitude. Head nods. *'What?'* hand fronting.

  Play your theme tune when you need a boost of self-belief – and do believe the hype :)

- If you're feeling down, compare what's happening with what could be happening – e.g. how much worse the reality could be? Don't dwell on it – all you need is a quick thought blast of how much worse it could be, then enjoy the fact it isn't! See how things seem now.

- Replace the word 'should' with 'could'.

- Ordinary miracles and small delights.

  Keep an eye out for both. From the gravity that keeps us from floating away to the simple joy of putting on a fresh pair of socks.

- Rap The Fresh Prince of Bel Air theme tune acapella. The acapella bit is ESSENTIAL.

You'll probably start off with some attitude thinking I've got this, I've done it with the credits *ppsht* but one verse in as the confidence starts to waver as you listen to yourself it's so *eeessshh* that it's literally impossible to take yourself seriously after.

Boom (shake the room) – fresh new mood.

- At the end of day before bed, think of a few nice moments which happened during that day. However small the moments, you will go to bed seeing the good in the day and carry that nice perspective with you into sleep and into the next morning.

- Touch something old

  One of my favourite things ever when I need a perspective shift is the (sometimes sneaky) pleasure of touching really old things from history.

  Old city wall? Statues from bygone eras? Anything which has existed for an almost impossible to comprehend amount of time? Boom, perspective!

  Knowing you are touching something which has existed through empires, wondering who else has stood where you're standing… Perspective swoon.

- Anyone you find difficult – imagine them as a child. An innocent child looking for love and affection. We all began there, and everyone is doing their best with what they experienced in life.

- Comedy break

  Think of a favourite comedy show or comedian, or maybe one of your favourite sketches. Either find a short clip to watch or listen to or replay a little in your head. Feel the smile start to spread. Give yourself over to it completely – the absurd joy of laughter.

- Reality check

  Often used as a technique for lucid dreaming – here, to get a bit Matrix. A few times during the day, hold one of your hands up, palm facing inwards, then take a finger from your other hand, and imagine that if you pushed the finger against the palm of your other hand, it would go through your hand. Then slowly watch as you bring your finger to the palm, still imagining it could be a possibility.

  This little trippy test of reality opens our mind and reminds us of the ridiculous amazingness that we exist, as does the world we live in!

BONUS FACTS! :)

- In the history of the Earth, we're closer to the Tyrannosaurus rex than the T.rex is to the Stegosaurus.

- Smaller animals experience time differently than we do. To tiny animals, larger animals appear to be in slow motion.

- NASA scientists have discovered stars that are cool enough to touch.

- According to astronauts' space smells like seared steak, hot metal, and welding fumes.

- There is a planet where it rains glass, sideways.

- One million Earths can fit inside the Sun.

- On Jupiter and Saturn, it rains diamonds.

- Approximately 70% of the universe is dark energy, and 25% is dark matter; both are invisible, even with our powerful telescopes. This means we have only seen 5% of the universe from Earth.

- When you sit in a chair, you are not actually sitting there, but levitating above it at a height of one angstrom (a hundred millionth of a centimetre).

- If you unravelled all of the DNA in your body, it would span 34 billion miles, reaching to Pluto (2.66 billion miles away) and back ... 13 times.

Printed in Great Britain
by Amazon